Witness History Series

THE INDUSTRIAL REVOLUTION

Nigel Smith

Titles in this series

The Arab-Israeli Conflict
Blitzkrieg!
Britain between the Wars
Britain since 1945
China since 1945
The Cold War
The Home Front
The Industrial Revolution
The Origins of the First World War
The Russian Revolution
South Africa since 1948
The Third Reich
Towards European Unity
The United Nations
The USA since 1945
War in the Trenches

Cover illustration: The membership certificate for an early Victorian trade union.

First published in 1990 by
Wayland (Publishers) Limited
61 Western Road, Hove
East Sussex BN3 1JD, England

Editor: Mike Hirst
Designer: Joyce Chester
Consultant: Brian Turner, Head of Economics and Politics, King's School Canterbury; Examiner for the Oxford and Cambridge Schools' Examination Board.

British Library Cataloguing in Publication Data
Smith, Nigel
  The industrial revolution. – (Witness history).
  1. Great Britain. Industrialization, history
  I. Title II. Series
  338.0941

ISBN 1–85210–867–3

Typeset by R. Gibbs & N. Taylor, Wayland
Printed by G.Canale & C.S.p.A., Turin
Bound by A.G.M., France

Contents

The eve of the Industrial Revolution

THE INDUSTRIAL REVOLUTION, which took place between 1750 and 1850, was a period of dramatic change in British history. One Victorian writer, looking back in 1846, said that, within the space of a single lifetime, there had been, 'the greatest advance in civilization that can be found recorded in the annals of mankind.'[1] There were enormous changes in the ways that people lived, the work they did and the way that the country was governed. From being a small, rural nation, Britain became one of the wealthiest and most powerful countries in the world.

In 1750, around six million people lived in England and Wales. London was the one big city, with a population of half a million. Only two other towns, Bristol and Norwich, had more than 20,000 inhabitants. Most people lived in the countryside, in villages or small towns. The great majority of them worked in agriculture, using long-established, traditional farming methods to get a living from the land. Communications were slow and the fastest means of travel, by horse, was expensive and uncomfortable. The cost of transporting goods and raw materials made trade difficult.

Some people did earn a living by manufacturing goods, though industry was very different from today. Most goods were produced in people's homes under what is known as the 'domestic system'. Many families combined work on the land with spinning and weaving cloth in their cottages, and the manufacture of woollen cloth was the most important and widespread industry. Iron and coal were two other long-established, but still small, industries. Coal mines were never very deep and rarely employed more than thirty miners. Before the

Water wheels were an important source of power before the coming of the steam-engine. However, life in pre-industrial Britain was not always as idyllic as this scene suggests. Poverty, hardship and sometimes even starvation were common.

◀ The world's first iron bridge at Coalbrookdale (1779) symbolized the new age of industrialization. Soon horses and donkeys were to be superseded by machines.

▶ Before the introduction of the factory system, most cloth was manufactured inside the workers' cottages. The domestic workers enjoyed some independence but worked long hours to make a living.

development of the steam-engine, the only sources of power were water wheels, windmills or horses.

The Industrial Revolution was to change the face of Britain completely. The steam-engine, railways and canals, factories and new ways of farming all had an enormous impact on people's lives. By 1851, there were eighteen million Britons, and the majority of them lived and worked, not in villages, but in towns and cities.

Historians still hotly debate the benefits and disadvantages of industrialization. Conditions were certainly not perfect before the Industrial Revolution; life for most people was harsh, and bad harvests or severe winters could cause widespread distress. After 1750, the overall wealth of the nation increased greatly. Yet the Industrial Revolution did not affect everyone in the same way. Changes in farming meant that more food was grown, but not everyone in the countryside shared in the new prosperity. Industrialization itself produced new social problems which took time to reform. The ways in which nineteenth-century Britons tackled these problems determined how the country has developed today.

1
POPULATION AND AGRICULTURE
Population growth

THE POPULATION OF BRITAIN increased rapidly between 1750 and 1850. These are the figures for England and Wales[2]:

Year	Population	Percentage Increase
1700	5.5 million (estimated)	
1750	6.5 million (estimated)	18%
1801	9 million (census)	39%
1851	18 million (census)	100%

Historians do not agree about the specific causes of the population growth, but it is clear that two main factors were at work: the rising birth rate and the falling death rate.

For a variety of reasons people lived longer and the death rate fell significantly. Plagues, such as the bubonic plague which killed large numbers of people in 1665, had been eliminated with the unexplained disappearance of the plague-carrying black rat. There were improvements in medical knowledge, such as the discovery of a vaccine against smallpox. Personal cleanliness improved too. What can you tell from these statistics for soap production?

Production of Soap in Tonnes [3]

1800	25,401	1830	50,294
1810	34,545	1840	88,903
1820	37,573	1850	96,524

Health also improved as a consequence of the cotton clothing produced by new textile mills. It could be washed easily and replaced some of the old, heavy and often germ-infested woollen garments.

In spite of these improvements, filthy conditions were common in the industrial towns and often there were no sewers or clean water supplies. Yet during the Industrial Revolution people did become more aware of the connection between cleanliness and good

By 1801, the south was no longer the most densely populated area of the country.

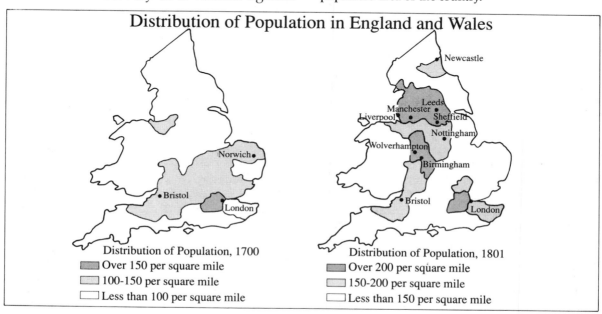

Distribution of Population in England and Wales

Distribution of Population, 1700
- Over 150 per square mile
- 100-150 per square mile
- Less than 100 per square mile

Distribution of Population, 1801
- Over 200 per square mile
- 150-200 per square mile
- Less than 150 per square mile

Thomas Malthus warned of disaster if the population continued to grow. Insufficient food would result in starvation and universal misery.

health. 'Cleanliness is indeed next to godliness', proclaimed the eighteenth-century preacher John Wesley.[4]

Another reason for the declining death rate was the improved diet of ordinary people. Agricultural changes and good harvests reduced the price of food and childbearing women in particular were better able to rear their children.

A rise in the birth rate also contributed to the population explosion. The falling death rate meant that more young people survived to have children of their own. There is also evidence that, on average, people began to marry younger and have larger families than before.

Even by 1850, the population of Britain was still small compared with today. Yet many middle-class people were frightened by the sudden increase in population. In his influential *Essay on the Principle of Population* (1798), the Revd Thomas Malthus warned that the population would rapidly outstrip resources and famine would follow:

> *It may safely be pronounced that population, when unchecked, goes on doubling itself every twenty-five years. Considering the present average state of the earth, the means of subsistence could not possibly be made to increase this quickly.*[5]

Malthus's pessimistic theory was used to discourage the poor from having large families by practising 'moral restraint'. However, in Britain, Malthus's predictions never came true. Industrial and agricultural changes and more imported food meant that Britain could support the growing population and even improve the standard of living throughout the nineteenth century.

The enclosure movement

In 1750 a great deal of land, particularly in the eastern counties of England, was still farmed on the open-field system. In a typical open-field village there were three huge fields, in addition to common land which everyone used for grazing animals. Each farmer had strips of land in each of the fields. Two fields were cultivated every year while the third field remained unused, or fallow, so that it could regain its fertility. This is a typical three-field crop rotation system:

	First Year	Second Year	Third Year
Field One	Wheat	Barley	Fallow
Field Two	Barley	Fallow	Wheat
Field Three	Fallow	Wheat	Barley

Although it had been used for centuries, this system of farming was inefficient and discouraged the use of new machines and ways of farming. Everyone had to grow the same crops and leave a third of the land unused each year. It was also difficult for farmers to work on many small pieces of land spread across the village.

Since the sixteenth century, rich farmers had gradually been buying land from their neighbours to make modern, enclosed fields. By the eighteenth century, the increased demand for food for the growing population encouraged landowners to enclose even more fields to create efficient, productive and profitable farms.

It was also possible to enclose whole villages by Acts of Parliament. Commissioners would visit a village to check everyone's claim to the land, divide it up and settle any disputes. By the end of the eighteenth century more and more villages

Some villages in Britain had been farmed according to the three-field system since the early Middle Ages.

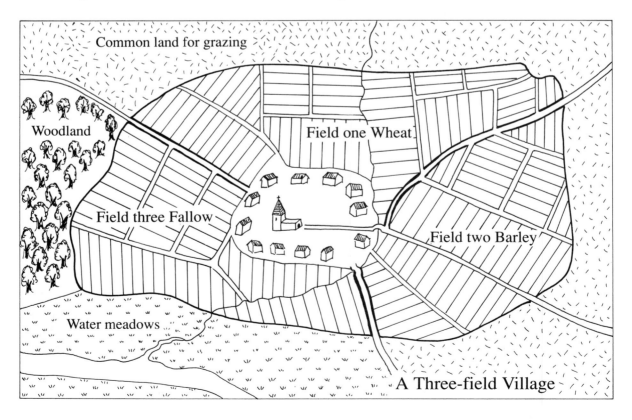

Common land for grazing

Woodland

Field one Wheat

Field three Fallow

Field two Barley

Water meadows

A Three-field Village

The new, enclosed farms required fewer labourers. Some poorer families, who had depended on the common land, were forced to seek work in the towns.

were being enclosed in this way, as the figures on the chart to the right show.[6]

Enclosures were certainly a major cause of increased food production. Arthur Young, an agricultural journalist, claimed that enclosure benefited everyone in society:

> *On the whole, the measure has been beneficial to every party: the land produces more corn; the farmers are in better circumstances; the poor have more bread and are better employed.*[7]

However, poor people could also suffer hardship because of enclosures. During enclosure, it was expensive to survey land, draw up plans and construct new fences and hedges. Those villagers unable to afford the high cost or prove their legal right to the land were forced to give up land that their families may have farmed for centuries. They also lost their right to graze animals on common land that was enclosed. After enclosure, some people who had previously farmed their own land were forced to look for work as agricultural labourers on the new, bigger farms, or even move to the industrial towns.

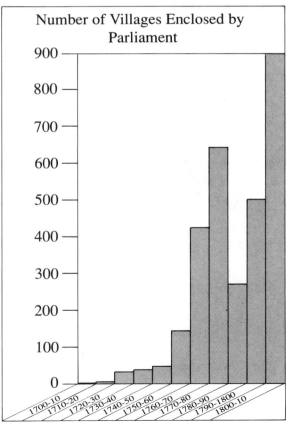

Number of Villages Enclosed by Parliament

Improvements in agriculture

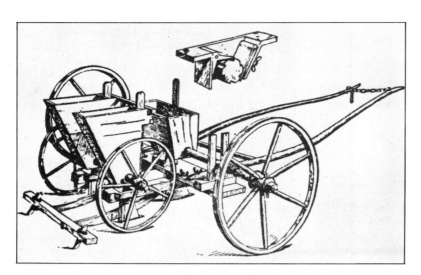

Jethro Tull's drill used only one eighth of the seed that was used by hand sowing. The drill produced straight rows and placed the seed at just the right depth and distance apart.

As farming became more profitable during the eighteenth century, farmers began to invest in new equipment and farming methods to increase the yield from their land. The growing population provided a ready market and enclosure made it easier for big farms to develop. The wars with France (1793–1815), when food imports virtually ceased, also boosted profits and investment in agriculture. New ideas were eagerly seized by farmers who sought to maximize the profitability of their farms.

The eighteenth century saw the introduction of new machines such as the seed drill, invented by Jethro Tull in 1701. It enabled farmers to sow seeds in straight rows, rather than by the old system of throwing seeds over the ground by hand, which was very wasteful. In Norfolk, Viscount 'Turnip' Townshend developed new types of crop rotation. Instead of leaving land fallow, he used a four-course crop rotation, planting turnips and clover which actually enrich the soil with vital nitrates. The turnips could be fed to animals which in turn further enriched the soil with manure.

The quality of livestock also improved. Robert Bakewell showed how to improve the weight of animals by selective breeding, allowing only the biggest and fittest animals to mate with each other. Bakewell stressed the quantity of meat produced rather than the quality, and the price of meat fell so that more people could afford it. What do you think Bakewell meant by this comment?

> *I do not breed mutton for gentlemen but for the public.*[8]

What do these figures tell us about the success of selective breeding?

Average Weight of Animals Taken to Market [9]

	1710	1795
Sheep	17 kg	36 kg
Cows	23 kg	68 kg
Bulls	168 kg	363 kg

What do you think was the effect of this increased meat production on the diet and health of the people?

These changes in farming are sometimes referred to as the Agricultural Revolution, although the process was probably too gradual to be a real 'revolution'. However, increased production of food was vital to industrial development, and factory towns could not have expanded so rapidly without additional supplies of cheap food.

These were some of the results of farming improvements:

- *More food for people in the towns.*
- *More fodder for cattle during the winter increased the supply of fresh meat all the year round.*
- *Farming became more businesslike and profitable.*

By 1815 most farmers were keen to use new methods and equipment and to run their farms as businesses. More land was farmed than ever before, some of it reclaimed from marshland, as almost any land could be used profitably to grow crops. Modern farmers, said one observer, deserved the title 'Great Improver': 'a title more deserving of distinction than that of a great general or a great minister.'[10]

▶ Robert Bakewell pioneered new methods of breeding which increased the amount of meat on each animal and so reduced the price of food.

▼ Cattle breeding became more profitable and farmers attended agricultural shows to buy, sell or simply admire the prize-winners. They could also exchange new ideas about farming at these shows.

2

REVOLUTION IN INDUSTRY
Causes of industrialization

BRITAIN WAS THE FIRST NATION in the world to become industrialized. Out of the inventions and economic growth of the Industrial Revolution grew the wealth that, during the nineteenth century, established Britain as the pre-eminent world power.

In the late eighteenth century certain essential ingredients came together to make the Industrial Revolution possible. The growing population provided both workers for industry and consumers to buy the new manufactured goods. Britain's considerable advantages were described in this way by a nineteenth-century writer:

> *Every facility seems at hand for starting us on a manufacturing career . . . Those metals which are of the greatest utility, and the coal which is requisite in working them, are distributed conveniently, and in inexhaustible abundance . . . we have a greater number of capacious harbours, as compared with the extent of land surface, than any other nation.*[11]

Britain was also fortunate to be an island nation whose trade and industry were rarely troubled by invasions. No wars had taken

British ships dominated international trade and British ports flourished. Bristol in particular profited from the slave trade and the import of American tobacco.

▲ Richard Arkwright was one of the first entrepreneurs to invest in new methods of mass production. His success encouraged others.

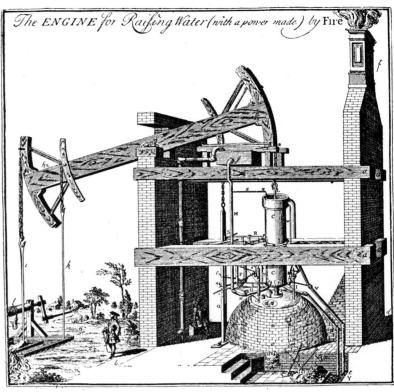

The ENGINE for Raiſing Water (with a power made) by Fire

▶ Newcomen's revolutionary steam-engine was first used to pump water from coal mines. Later improvements made the steam-engine the driving force of the entire industrial process.

place in England and Wales since the Civil War in the mid-seventeenth century.

Another important requirement was wealth, or capital, to invest in building up new industries and to encourage experimentation in machines. Rich merchants and ship owners who had profited from international trade, including the slave trade to the West Indies and North America, had money available to invest. Many of them were keen to encourage the production of goods which they knew would boost British exports. In particular, the opening up of the USA offered plentiful cotton as a new, cheap raw material, while also providing a growing market for British manufactured goods. The new entrepreneurs, prepared to take risks in the hope of profits, vigorously promoted new businesses using the latest technology.

Various inventions, especially the steam-engine, played a vital role in industrial development. In the iron and textile industries, technological advances made

mass production in factories possible for the first time. In turn, the prospect of boosting production and profits was a strong incentive both for investors and experimenters to pursue new and improved means of manufacturing. Inventions then stimulated further development and innovation. The textile and iron industries were quickest to adopt new ideas, but by the mid-nineteenth century most industries, even the small ones, were adopting the new technology.

Rapid industrialization increased the output of goods, made many people very rich and established Britain as the wealthiest nation in the world. Other countries had, at first, lacked the particular combination of resources and opportunities that enabled Britain to lead with the Industrial Revolution. However, in time other countries did begin to take up British ideas. They bought and copied British machines and inventions, and so moved towards becoming industrialized societies themselves.

The steam-engine

Crucial to the development of industry and the factory system was the invention and improvement of the steam-engine; it was 'the pivot on which industry swung into the modern age'.[12] Compared with water wheels and windmills, the steam-engine gave industry two new key advantages. First, it provided reliable and consistent power to operate mass production in factories. It also meant that factories no longer had to be located where there was a fast-moving river to provide water power.

It had long been understood that there was power in steam, and in 1712 Thomas Newcomen built a steam-engine to pump water out of coal mines. In 1775 James Watt improved on Newcomen's design, and in 1781 he adapted the steam-engine to rotary power. This important improvement used a series of cogs and wheels so that the engine could turn a wheel. By using a driving belt an engine could also work a factory machine.

Watt's invention was a dramatic breakthrough. Soon important industrialists had installed the new rotary steam-engine, and its use was pioneered by people such as Richard Arkwright, the textile manufacturer. John Wilkinson of the Coalbrookdale Iron Company and Josiah Wedgwood, who built up a famous pottery business, also put steam-engines to work in their factories. Historians are in no doubt as to the long-term importance of the rotary engine:

> With the perfection and adoption of a power engine, made of iron and steel and using coal, England had completed the first stage of a profound revolutionary process. Man was no longer dependent on the natural sources of power.[13]

James Watt improved the steam-engine so that it could turn wheels and drive machinery in the new mills and factories.

Although steam had many advantages, the introduction of the steam-engine was gradual. It was not until after the 1820s that the real breakthrough came for steam power, with the introduction of more factory machinery and steam-powered transport, the railways and steamships. For a long time many factories continued to use water and wind power because of the heavy expense involved in installing steam-engines. The first steam-engine to be used in London in 1786 cost £60,000 – a great deal of money in the eighteenth century. Only the very wealthiest and the most ambitious manufacturers could afford these new machines.

Evidence of the fairly small number of steam-engines in use by 1800 comes from these figures for engines installed by Boulton and Watt, who were the main steam-engine manufacturers[14]:

Number of Engines Supplied before 1800		Total Horsepower
Cotton Mills	84	1382
Foundries & Forges	28	618
Copper Mines	22	440
Collieries	30	380
Canals	18	261
Water Works	13	241

Compared with these steam-engines, there would still have been many thousands of windmills and water wheels in use.

For those who did adopt steam power the rewards in increased production and profit were very great. In time mass-produced steam-engines transformed all of industry as well as transport.

In Watt's steam-engine, a coal fire heated the water to create steam. The steam then passed into a cylinder, where it pushed a piston upwards. As the piston moved up, the steam was allowed to pass into a second cylinder, where it was condensed by cold water. Air pressure then pushed the piston back down into the main cylinder again.

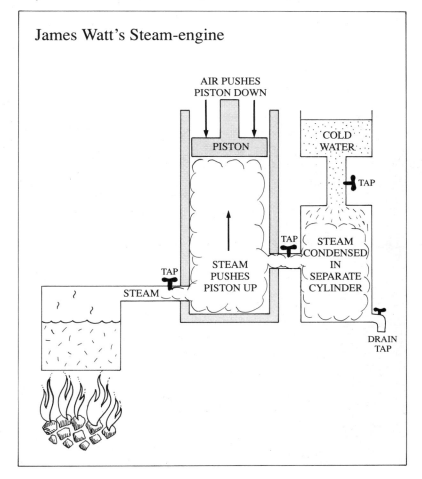

James Watt's Steam-engine

AIR PUSHES PISTON DOWN

PISTON

COLD WATER

TAP

STEAM PUSHES PISTON UP

TAP

STEAM CONDENSED IN SEPARATE CYLINDER

TAP

STEAM

TAP

DRAIN TAP

The textile industry

Even before the Industrial Revolution, Britain had a long-established textile industry. In many parts of the country, woollen cloth had been manufactured for centuries in the domestic system; whole families worked together, spinning and weaving in their homes to produce cloth. However, during the eighteenth century, there were enormous changes in the textile industry.

Alongside the woollen industry, a new industry grew up, making cotton cloth. Raw cotton, from the colonies in North America and India, was cheap and in plentiful supply. Cotton clothes also had advantages over woollen ones. They were lighter and more comfortable to wear. Cotton was easier to wash and therefore more hygienic. It could also be produced more cheaply.

During the late eighteenth century, there were a number of inventions that made it possible to produce cotton cloth quickly and in bulk:

- *1764 James Hargreaves's spinning jenny. This machine could spin up to 120 threads at the same time.*
- *1769 Richard Arkwright's water-frame spinning machine. It was driven by water power and therefore could only be used in factories.*
- *1775 Richard Arkwright's carding machine. It combed out the fibres of the cotton.*
- *1779 Samuel Compton's spinning mule. This machine could produce finer and stronger thread.*
- *1785 Edward Cartwright's power loom. This loom was powered by a water wheel or steam-engine and could only be used inside a factory.*

These inventions led to a huge increase in cotton production:

Annual Cotton Production (in Tonnes) [15]

1760	8,128 tonnes
1800	25,400 tonnes
1830	101,600 tonnes

The new inventions also meant that it was easier and more economical to produce both cotton and woollen cloth, not in people's homes, but in large factories. Richard Arkwright is credited as being the founder of

The spinning jenny was one machine that revolutionized textile production and replaced the old-fashioned spinning wheels used in domestic industry.

the factory system; he built the first water-powered cotton mills in 1771 at Cromford, Derbyshire.

Encouraged by the damp climate (which made it easier to spin thread) and closeness to the port of Liverpool, the cotton industry became centred on Lancashire. New mills sprang up in the towns of Manchester, Rochdale and Bolton.

The factory system and the speed with which it developed and spread amazed many people. What was this nineteenth-century commentator's attitude to the new ways of manufacturing cloth?

> *The steam-engine had no precedent, the spinning jenny is without ancestry, the mule and the power loom entered on no prepared heritage: they sprang into sudden existence like Minerva from the brain of Jupiter.*[16]

Yet not everyone welcomed the new textile machinery. It spelt the end of the domestic system of cloth manufacture, and the power loom in particular put many handloom weavers out of work. People who had earlier worked in their own homes were now forced to look for jobs in the new factories.

Arkwright's textile mill opened at Cromford, Derbyshire in 1771. It ushered in the factory system that during the next fifty years replaced the domestic system of production.

The coal industry

Coal was the essential source of power for the Industrial Revolution. Most of the new industrial processes depended on a cheap, plentiful supply of the fuel. Steam-engines, railways and steamships all consumed vast quantities of coal and more was also needed to heat the increasing number of homes. Fortunately Britain possessed large deposits of coal, and production increased rapidly:

Coal Production in Tonnes [17]

1700	2,032,000
1779	6,096,000
1800	10,160,000
1830	23,368,000
1850	66,040,000

What do these figures suggest to you about the importance of coal to industrial development?

New industries developed in those areas that were closest to supplies of coal.

Although large deposits of coal existed, serious technical problems had to be overcome before it could be extracted from the ground. As the mines went deeper to reach new coal seams, flooding became a major problem. It was solved only by using steam-powered pumping-engines; Watt's steam-engine, in use after 1775, powered the first really effective pumping equipment that was able to drain the deepest mines.

Mines were also prone to build-ups of poisonous and explosive gases. Additional ventilation shafts were dug, but they could only partially remove the gases. Explosive methane gas in particular was dangerous for miners, who had to work by candle light. This problem, of providing light without igniting the gases, was not finally solved until the invention of a safety lamp in 1815.

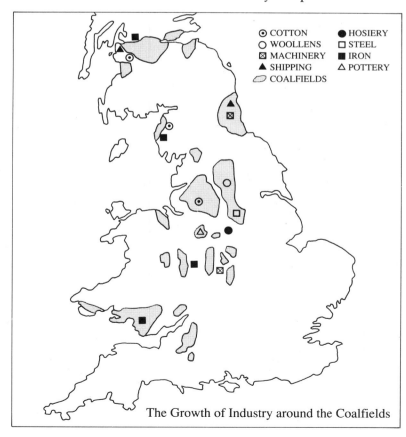

⊙ COTTON   ● HOSIERY
○ WOOLLENS   □ STEEL
⊠ MACHINERY   ■ IRON
▲ SHIPPING   △ POTTERY
⬭ COALFIELDS

The Growth of Industry around the Coalfields

◄ Men, women and children worked long hours in dangerous and difficult conditions to produce the coal that fuelled the Industrial Revolution. Children were employed to haul huge baskets of coal along narrow tunnels in total darkness.

▼ The miner's safety lamp was invented by Humphrey Davy. A wire gauze prevented the lamp's flame from coming into contact with highly explosive gas.

Even transporting coal to the surface was hazardous, though new machinery gradually made this process safer too. Steam-powered winding gear eventually replaced the ladders up which women struggled to carry huge wicker baskets of coal. Steel cable also replaced the ropes that were liable to break as the coal or miners were hauled to the surface. In spite of these inventions, actually extracting the coal underground still relied on the pick and shovel, and sheer hard physical work of the miners.

The conditions in the mines, where men, women and children were employed, were grim and dangerous. It is estimated that even by the 1840s, accidents killed five out of every thousand underground workers each year, and many others were injured. This fatal accident occurred in 1772:

A woman employed in putting at South Biddick was riding up one of the pits when the other hook, in passing, caught her clothes. The weight of the rope forced her out of the loop, and she fell to the bottom of the shaft.[18]

What does this account suggest about standards of safety in the mines?

Sir Humphrey Davy, Bart.

INVENTOR

OF

THE

SAFETY LAMP

The new iron industry

For centuries, iron had been smelted (extracted from iron ore) in Britain using charcoal, a kind of burnt wood. However, a growing wood shortage made charcoal more difficult to obtain and, during the seventeenth century, many ironmasters had unsuccessfully experimented with the use of coal instead of charcoal for smelting. Then, in 1709, Abraham Darby began to smelt iron ore successfully in his Coalbrookdale foundry, using coke which was produced from coal. Darby's new smelting process was the foundation upon which the British iron industry was to expand.

Gradually other processes were developed to improve the quality of iron production. Demand for iron increased as it became clear that factory machinery was better if it was made out of iron instead of wood. In 1784 Henry Cort devised the puddling process

Coalbrookdale became a major centre of iron production. The Darby family developed new methods to mass produce the cheaper and stronger iron that other industries relied on.

which made it possible to manufacture purer iron than ever before using coke furnaces. Mass production of cheap iron became possible, and there was a considerable increase in production:

British Pig Iron Output in Tonnes[19]

1720	25,400	1830	687,832
1788	69,088	1840	1,418,336
1796	127,000	1847	2,030,984
1806	247,904	1852	2,744,216
1823	462,280		

The Darby family's iron business flourished, and by 1800 a quarter of all iron produced was being smelted at

Coalbrookdale. This description is by a visitor in the 1790s. Do you think he was impressed by what he saw?

> *The immense furnace stood in the centre of a large area walled around, communicating with each side of which was a colossal pair of bellows, whose alternate blasts, with a noise like the incessant roaring of heavy ordnance, excited an intense heat, which had to be kept up night and day for a considerable time to separate the metal from the stone, and to reduce it to a state of fusion.*[20]

The world's first iron bridge was constructed across the River Severn by Abraham Darby III in 1779, and in 1791 an iron bridge was exported to Holland. These bridges demonstrated that iron had many uses that people had never thought of before. Coalbrookdale pots and pans became world famous, and parts for steam-engines, railway locomotives and rails were also manufactured. Railway expansion in particular depended on the availability of vast quantities of cheap iron. In 1839–40 Coalbrookdale also supplied wrought-iron plates for the first large iron steamship to use a screw propeller, Brunel's SS *Great Britain*.

The methods developed at Coalbrookdale were adapted and improved in other parts of the country such as South Wales and Scotland, where there were good coal supplies. Just as coal production encouraged industrial growth, the great increase in cheap iron also stimulated other manufacturing industries which needed iron for machinery and products.

By 1830 there were 200 steamships operating from British ports. Brunel's SS *Great Britain*, with its screw propeller, can still be seen today, preserved at Wapping Dock in Bristol.

Factory conditions

The introduction of the factory system had a profound effect on people's lives, and by 1839 there were 419,560 factory workers; 192,887 of them were under eighteen and 242,296 were female.[21] In many of the new factories, both adults and children had to work for long hours in harsh and unhealthy conditions, often subject to a brutal factory discipline. This is how one writer described the life of a factory worker in 1818:

> *Locked up in factories eight stories high, he has no relaxation till the ponderous engine stops; and then he goes home to get refreshed for the next day; no time for sweet association with his family; they are all alike fatigued and exhausted.*[22]

Work in the factories could be as long as fourteen hours a day, starting at six in the morning for six days a week. Factory owners enforced strict rules and levied fines against

Young children were employed in the cotton mills, often doing dangerous work. What job is the young boy on the right of the picture doing? Why was it dangerous?

those people who broke them. Trade unions were weak or illegal and workers could rarely organize to improve their conditions.

Factories (especially the cotton mills) were often damp, with poor ventilation. Sanitation usually consisted of no more than a bucket in the corner. What effect might these conditions have had upon the health of the workers? Dr Loudon, a government commissioner, made this report in 1844:

> *I think it has been clearly proved that children have been worked a most unreasonable and cruel length of time daily . . . the consequence is that many have died prematurely, and others are afflicted for life with defective constitutions.*[23]

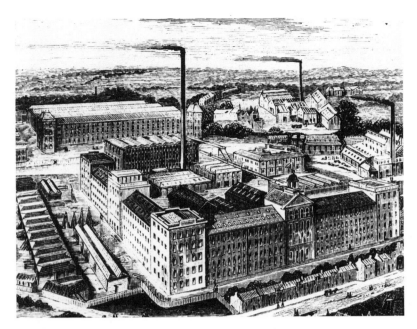

◀ Many domestic workers, such as the weavers, saw their traditional livelihood destroyed by the new factories. Adults and their children often had to accept work under whatever conditions their employers offered.

▼ Friedrich Engels was one of the first people to acknowledge the miseries of factory work in his *Conditions of the Working Class in England*. Although this influential book was based on Engels' experiences in Manchester, it was not published in English until the end of the nineteenth century.

In spite of the treatment of factory workers, governments were very reluctant to pass regulations of hours and conditions. They maintained a policy of *laissez-faire*, or not intervening in trade and industry. In 1812 the prime minister, Lord Liverpool, justified this policy, saying; ' It is undoubtably true that the less commerce and manufacture are meddled with, the more likely they are to prosper.'[24]

The factory system did have enormous benefits for industrial production and contributed greatly to economic growth. It is also true that, during the Industrial Revolution, factory wages were better than those in agriculture and many town workers had a higher standard of living than their counterparts in the countryside. Historians are faced with the question of whether these benefits outweighed the human suffering caused by the factory system.

One consequence of the factory system is quite clear. A new social group developed – the industrial working class. In the new towns, large numbers of people belonged to this group. During the nineteenth century, they were to protest more and more against the unfairness of British industrial society and demand reform.

Die Lage
der
arbeitenden Klasse
in
England.

Nach eigner Anschauung und authentischen Quellen
von
Friedrich Engels.

Leipzig.
Druck und Verlag von Otto Wigand.
1845.

3
REVOLUTION IN TRANSPORT
Roads and canals

THE TRANSPORT of bulky raw materials and finished goods was a serious problem for eighteenth-century industrialists. There had been some improvements in the condition of main roads with the formation of turnpike companies which charged tolls for the use of roads. Yet turnpike trusts improved fewer than half of the roads, and travel for most people remained difficult and dangerous. One solution was to make more rivers navigable and construct a canal network which linked the major industrial areas with ports and cities.

James Brindley's successful construction of a canal (1759–1761) for the Duke of Bridgewater, linking the coal mines of Worsley to Manchester, quickly proved the value of canals. The price of coal in Manchester was halved and Bridgewater's profits soared. A programme of canal building soon followed. Brindley's own goal was to create a 'Grand Cross' scheme, which

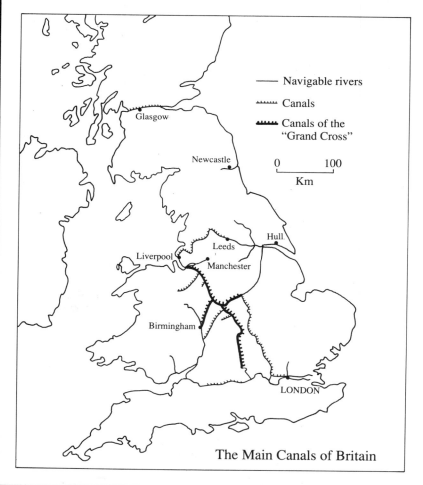

Navigable rivers

Canals

Canals of the "Grand Cross"

0   100
Km

Glasgow

Newcastle

Hull

Leeds

Liverpool

Manchester

Birmingham

LONDON

The Main Canals of Britain

James Brindley overcame obstacles in canal building by the use of locks and aqueducts. His canal for the Duke of Bridgewater encouraged 'canal mania' and the construction of an extensive inland waterway network.

would link the four great ports of London, Liverpool, Bristol and Hull. This 'Grand Cross' canal network was finally completed after Brindley's death in 1793.

Canals were ideal for the cheap transportation of bulky goods such as coal, fertilizers and building materials, and for finished manufactured goods. The pottery industry flourished with the use of canals to transport its fragile finished product. Inland coalfields expanded and prospered with the help of canals. Thriving new canal towns such as Stourport and Runcorn grew up. Thousands of people obtained work building the canals. The new canal companies themselves were often highly profitable and produced a good financial return for investors.

Although the canal era lasted only from 1760 to 1830, canals were vitally important to industrial growth. This is one historian's assessment of their significance:

> The canals must be reckoned a major element in British industrial development before the railways . . . the assistance given to the heavy industries, such as coal and iron, and to the building and constructional industries was great . . . it is hard to see how much of the contemporary growth in towns and industries could have taken place without them.[25]

However, although they had advantages over the roads for the carriage of bulky goods, canals had several flaws. In winter they might freeze over and in summer dry up. They were difficult and expensive to build in hilly areas, and they were extremely slow. In the end, they were superseded by another new, revolutionary form of transport: the railways.

The railway age

The impact of the railways on nineteenth-century Britain was so great that the period is often described as the 'Railway Age'. The engineering, technological and iron-making skills of the Industrial Revolution combined in the construction of this new means of transport. What can you tell from the chart on the opposite page about the speed with which railways developed?

In 1808 Richard Trevithick demonstrated his *Catch-Me-Who-Can* steam locomotive in London. Yet it was not until George Stephenson and his son, Robert, built their successful locomotive for the Stockton to Darlington railway in 1825 that the potential of steam locomotion was realized. Their railway between the cities of Liverpool and Manchester, with its locomotive, the *Rocket*, opened in 1830.

The Stephensons' success encouraged rapid investment in railway construction, and by the 1840s 'railway mania' had taken hold. The bulk of the network was completed by the 1860s, and Victorians were enormously impressed by this great achievement that transformed their lives. This observation made in 1842 expresses contemporary feelings:

> *Railroad travelling is a delightful improvement of human life. The early Scotchman scratches himself in the morning mists of the North, and has his porridge in Piccadilly before the setting of the sun . . . Everything is near, everything is immediate – time, distance and delay are abolished.*[26]

For the first time it was easy to travel in pursuit of employment, for pleasure or on business. In 1848 W.H. Smith started sending London newspapers to Scotland, and the

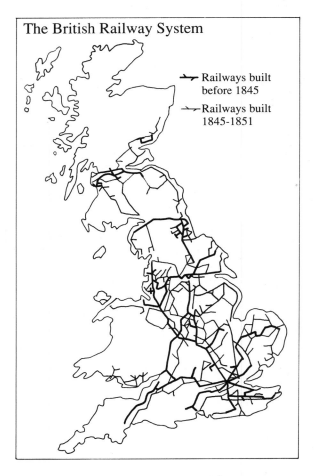

The British Railway System

→ Railways built before 1845

→ Railways built 1845-1851

Penny Post, which began in 1840, switched from stage-coaches to railways. Reasonably priced travel for the working classes was guaranteed by the 1844 Railway Act which required every railway company to send at least one train a day along each line, stopping at every station and charging just one penny per mile. Consider how difficult a journey from Scotland to London must have been before the railways were built. Compare these journey times:[27]

	Stage-coach 1836	Train 1844	Train 1876
London-Birmingham	11 hours	8 hours 55 mins	2 hours 40 mins
London-Hull	18 hours	11 hours 5 mins	5 hours 20 mins
London-Newcastle	30 hours 20 mins	12 hours 15 mins	6 hours 5 mins

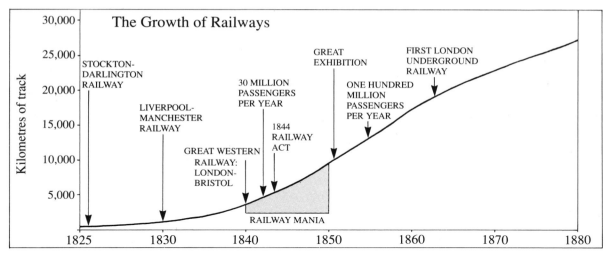

The Growth of Railways

Kilometres of track

STOCKTON-DARLINGTON RAILWAY

LIVERPOOL-MANCHESTER RAILWAY

GREAT WESTERN RAILWAY: LONDON-BRISTOL

30 MILLION PASSENGERS PER YEAR

1844 RAILWAY ACT

RAILWAY MANIA

GREAT EXHIBITION

ONE HUNDRED MILLION PASSENGERS PER YEAR

FIRST LONDON UNDERGROUND RAILWAY

Railways created a social revolution. The middle classes began to move out of town centres into new suburbs, commuting to their businesses. In the summer they visited new holiday resorts such as Blackpool and Southend. Fresh food could be transported easily, to the benefit of both farmers and townspeople.

Railways were also a strong impetus to further industrial growth; these were some of their important effects:

- *Reduced transport costs of raw materials and manufactured goods.*
- *Increased demand for coal, iron and building materials needed by the railways.*
- *Thousands of new jobs building and running railways.*

Yet even the railways had some critics. The reactionary Duke of Wellington was suspicious of them at first, fearing that they would encourage the workers to 'move about'![28]

Robert Stephenson's *Rocket* steam locomotive could travel at an average speed of 22 kph and even go as fast as 50 kph.

4
TWO NATIONS
The rich and the poor

THE HUGE INCREASE in national wealth, generated by economic growth, increased the gulf between rich and poor. In the countryside, farmers and landowners who were able to take advantage of enclosures added to their already considerable wealth; yet those people who lost their smallholdings and laboured on the land lived in great poverty. Successful new industries in the cities produced considerable and ever-growing profits for their owners; but factory workers received only a small share of the new wealth.

Many wealthy people took the convenient view that this social order had been ordained by God and should not be interfered with.

Until the 1830s, political power remained firmly in the hands of the rich, particularly the landed gentry. The 1834 Parliamentary Reform Act gave many middle-class men the right to vote, but without extending it to most, working-class, people. However, by the 1830s the new urban working class was beginning to demand better wages and conditions, social reform and the right to vote. Well-to-do people, recalling the French Revolution of 1789, were always nervous that such discontent might boil over into violence against them.

In 1845 a prominent Tory politician, Benjamin Disraeli, who was later to become prime minister, highlighted the gulf between

A wealthy social reformer visiting the slums. Most upper and middle-class people rarely experienced at first hand how the poor lived.

This illustration conveys the rather idealized view of Victorian middle-class life. The father is surrounded by his extensive family in their comfortable home. Why was there such a gulf between the rich and poor?

rich and poor. How might wealthy people have reacted to this extract from Disraeli's novel, *Sybil*, widely read among the middle and upper classes?

> '... Say what you like, our Queen reigns over the greatest nation that ever existed.'
> 'Which nation?' asked the younger stranger, 'for she reigns over two ... Two nations; between whom there is no intercourse and no sympathy; who are as ignorant of each other's habits, thoughts and feelings, as if they were dwellers in different zones, or inhabitants of different planets; who are formed by different breeding, are fed by a different food, are ordered by different manners, and are not governed by the same laws ... THE RICH AND THE POOR.'[29]

Disraeli's writing was controversial and the questions of poverty and the responsibilities of the rich were hotly debated. What kind of arguments might have taken place in the stately homes or London's

gentlemen's clubs at the time that *Sybil* was published? This is how one radical writer saw British society at the beginning of the nineteenth century:

> The workman is the source of all wealth. Who has raised all the food? The half-fed and impoverished labourer. Who spins all the yarn and makes all the cloth? The spinner and the weaver. Yet the labourer remains poor and destitute, while those who do not work are rich and possess abundance.[30]

Which groups of people would have been likely to agree with this writer?

The two most influential radical writers were Karl Marx and Friedrich Engels, Germans who lived and worked in England. Founders of communism, they believed that, eventually, the working classes in all industrialized countries would rise up against the upper classes, overthrow the social order and seize power for themselves.

New industrial towns

The 1851 population census showed that, for the first time, more than half of the population was living in urban areas. Some people were bewildered by this new phenomenon of large, industrial towns. One visitor to London in 1848 recorded:

> A town where a man may wander for hours without reaching the beginning of the end . . . is a strange thing. [31]

The rapid and unplanned growth of towns resulted in extensive slums where there was little regard for comfort or hygiene.

The new industrial towns were largely unplanned and consisted of jerry-built houses, thrown up as quickly and cheaply as possible. A few industrialists, such as Robert Owen in New Lanark, created model communities for their own workers. Yet in the early nineteenth century governments held to the policy of *laissez-faire* and refused to take any positive action to improve conditions. This is what the French writer, de Tocqueville, wrote after a visit to Manchester:

> Everything in the exterior appearance of the city attests the individual powers of man; nothing the directing power of society. At every turn human liberty shows its capricious creative force. There is no trace of the slow continuous action of government. [32]

Do you think de Tocqueville supported or opposed the policy of *laissez-faire*?

Other people were more outspoken in their criticism of conditions in towns. This description of Leeds appeared in the *Morning Chronicle* in 1849:

> Conceive acre on acre of little streets, run up without attention to plan or health – acre on acre of closely-built and thickly-peopled ground without a paving stone upon the surface, or an inch of sewer beneath, deep trodden – churned sloughs of mud forming the only thoroughfares – here and there an open space, used as the common-yard of the vicinity – in its centre, ash pits employed for dirtier purposes – privies, often ruinous, always horribly foul . . . [33]

Conditions such as these were degrading and, as well as disease and squalor, the towns became centres of crime and discontent. Many people sought solace in gin and beer drinking establishments.

The government did take some measures to improve conditions in towns. Edwin

Birmingham (above) in 1779 and (left) in 1850. It was one of the fastest-growing cities and its population increased from 71,000 in 1801 to 233,000 by 1851.

Chadwick, secretary of the Poor Law Commission, was one of the few energetic campaigners for improvement. His 1842 *Report into the Sanitary Condition of the Labouring Population* led to the formation of a short-lived Central Board of Health. After the creation of town councils in 1835, it was also possible for local authorities to take some measures to improve conditions. However, opposition to government action remained strong. *The Times* even attacked the Board of Health, saying that British people would not be bullied into reform:

> *Everywhere the Board's inspectors were arbitrary, insulting and expensive.*[34]

What did *The Times* mean by the words 'arbitrary' and 'insulting'? Who do you think was most afraid that reform would be 'expensive'?

Women workers

Up until recent times, women have rarely been accorded equal rights with men. A married woman's property and earnings automatically belonged to her husband and, before 1918, no women were allowed to vote. Women such as Mary Wollstonecraft, who in 1792 demanded greater equality in a book entitled *A Vindication of the Rights of Women*, were generally criticized and belittled.

Although nineteenth-century women remained, by and large, unequal with men, the Industrial Revolution had a profound effect upon the position of women in society. In particular, there were great changes in the kind of work they did.

Women had always been employed in domestic manufacturing, but they now began to go out of the home to work in the new factories. Factory owners realized that many jobs could be done by women and children

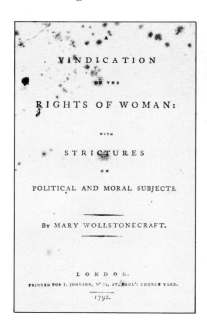

▲ The title page of Mary Wollstonecraft's *A Vindication of the Rights of Women*.

▶ Mary Wollstonecraft was far ahead of her time. Her argument that women should not always be physically and economically dependant on men received little support in 1792.

and that women could be paid lower wages than men. This extract is from an 1844 factory inspector's report:

> *A vast majority of the persons employed at night, and for long hours during the day, are females. Their labour is cheaper, and they are more easily induced to undergo severe bodily fatigue than men . . .*[35]

Look at this table of wages in a Lancashire cotton mill.[36]

Age	Number of Women Workers	Average Weekly Wages Women	Men
16–21	1,240	7s 3d	10s 2d
21–26	780	8s 5d	17s 2d
26–31	295	8s 7d	20s 4d

(12d = 1 shilling, 20 shillings = £1)

Notice the way that women's wages increased much less than men's as they grew older. Why do you think factory owners could get away with paying women lower wages than men?

Although women factory workers were clearly exploited, some historians have stressed the benefits of industrialization for

Factory owners preferred to employ women, and at times of high unemployment women were often the sole wage earners. How might their fathers and husbands have reacted to this?

women. For the first time, large numbers of women were actually earning an independent wage. Factory jobs gave women new opportunities outside the home and set them on a path to the greater political, social and economic equality of the twentieth century:

> *In the case of the single working woman, the most striking effect of the Industrial Revolution was her distinct gain in social and economic independence as a matter of course . . .*[37]

However, do you think that many of the women who laboured long hours in factories and mines appreciated their new-found 'independence'? Most women went out to work, not seeking greater opportunities, but because their families needed the extra money to survive. In the short term, were women any more independent if they had little real choice as to how they spent the wages they earned?

The Poor Law

During the early part of the Industrial Revolution, those people, such as the sick, the old and the unemployed, who could not support themselves, had to seek assistance from the local parish. After 1796, many parishes adopted the so-called Speenhamland system of poor relief (named after the village where it was introduced). It gave assistance to poor people according to the price of bread and the size of their family.

Unfortunately, the Speenhamland system was expensive. In 1803 expenditure on the poor was estimated to be £4 million; in 1818 it reached a peak of £8 million and it was still £6 million in 1832. Some people claimed that the system encouraged the poor to be lazy and rely on assistance. Moreover, some employers appeared deliberately to hold down wages in the knowledge that assistance would make up the rest.

In 1834, parliament passed the Poor Law Amendment Act to reform the system of poor relief. For the first time, central government

Do you think that the artist who drew this picture was trying to create a favourable or an unfavourable impression of a workhouse? Is this a 'place of wholesome restraint'?

took over responsibility for the poor. The new Poor Law was strongly influenced by Edwin Chadwick, a lawyer, who wanted it to be as inexpensive as possible. The government itself was following a policy of strict economy, reducing spending to keep taxation as low as possible. It accepted Chadwick's principles of the 'workhouse test' and 'less eligibility':

> By the workhouse system is meant having all relief through the workhouse, making this workhouse an uninviting place of wholesome restraint, preventing any of its inmates from going out or receiving visitors . . . disallowing beer and tobacco, and finding them work . . . [38]

What do you think Chadwick meant by the phrase, 'an uninviting place of wholesome restraint'?

To obtain any help from the government, poor people had to leave their homes and enter a workhouse. Life there was almost like that in a prison. People were forced to work long hours, and had virtually no freedom. The condition of the inmates was to be kept 'less eligible', that is, worse, than that of the poorest labourers outside. In the north, workhouses were even nicknamed 'Bastilles' after the notorious French prison. To deter the poor from seeking help, assistance was combined with virtual punishment.

Besides being cheap, the new Poor Law was based on the belief of many middle-class people that poor people were somehow responsible for their own misfortune. Poverty was seen as a disgrace brought on people by their own idleness or improvidence. Few people attempted to examine the root causes of poverty.

The harshness of the new Poor Law angered many working-class people. It was one of the main causes of the growing discontent among the poor of nineteenth-century Britain. It also encouraged the growth of working-class protest movements such as the Chartists and early trade unions.

At times of high unemployment anger against the Poor Law boiled over in riots and attacks on the hated workhouses.

5
PROTEST AND REFORM
Working-class discontent

INDUSTRIAL PROGRESS made some people very wealthy; it also caused unemployment and hardship for those whose traditional occupations were replaced by the new factories. Particularly during the Napoleonic Wars, when poor harvests coincided with high unemployment, strong protest movements developed.

Machine breaking in the textile trades was one expression of anger. Skilled workers smashed the new machines which were destroying their jobs. In 1811, armed groups of people who worked in the Midlands hosiery trade began to smash hundreds of stocking frames. Their leader was a shadowy figure called Ned Ludd, from whom the group took their name of Luddites. The Tory government, led by Spencer Perceval, responded by making machine breaking a capital offence, but the Luddites merely became more defiant, as this Luddite song demonstrates:

> *Welcome Ned Ludd, your case is good,*
> *Make Perceval your aim;*
> *For by this Bill 'tis understood*
> *It's death to break a frame.*
>
> *You might as well be hung for death*
> *As breaking a machine,*
> *So now, my lad, your sword unsheath,*
> *And make it sharp and keen.*[39]

The following year, Luddite attacks spread to west Yorkshire, where new machinery was causing unemployment among a group of

How does this view of working-class protesters contrast with the cartoon of the Peterloo Massacre opposite? What is the role of women in this picture?

skilled textile workers called croppers. Now the government responded severely. It sent troops to the area, and, after a Luddite attack on a mill, many Luddites were arrested. Seventeen Luddites were hanged and others were transported to Australia.

In 1819 there was further harsh government repression, this time after a peaceful protest. A mass meeting at St Peter's Field, Manchester, was broken up by armed cavalry; eleven people were killed and a further 420 were injured. The event was dubbed the 'Peterloo Massacre', in angry mockery of the great military victory at Waterloo four years earlier. Many people were appalled by the bloodshed, but the government defended the soldiers' action, as

What was the intention of this cartoon of the Peterloo Massacre? How does it portray the role of soldiers and the crowd? Do you think it is reliable historical evidence?

you can tell from this comment by one of their supporters:

> *I consider such meetings as that held at Manchester, to be nothing more or less than risings of the people; and I believe, that these risings of the people, if suffered to continue, would end in open rebellion.*[40]

What does this passage suggest about the attitudes of the ruling classes towards popular protest movements? Many wealthy people were frightened by the memory of the French Revolution of 1789.

After Peterloo the government reacted by introducing new laws, called the Six Acts, to silence unrest. Public meetings were strictly controlled, radical newspapers were banned and suspects could be held without trial, to speed up the legal system and make a quick example of any agitator.

The Great Reform Act

In 1831 only 440,000 men, out of a population of twenty-four million, had the right to vote. Landowners wielded considerable influence and parliament usually reflected the interests of the landowning classes. Middle-class men who wanted political influence, or wanted to become MPs, had to invest their industrial profits in land. The system was unjust and did not reflect the changing face of British society.

The majority of MPs represented the southern half of England, many from sparsely populated areas. Large industrial towns such as Sheffield and Manchester were unrepresented. 'Rotten boroughs', such as Old Sarum, where virtually no one lived any more, still returned two MPs, chosen by the local landowner. Some landowners controlled 'pocket boroughs', with just a

The 1832 Reform Act took MPs away from rotten and pocket boroughs to increase representation for the new industrial towns.

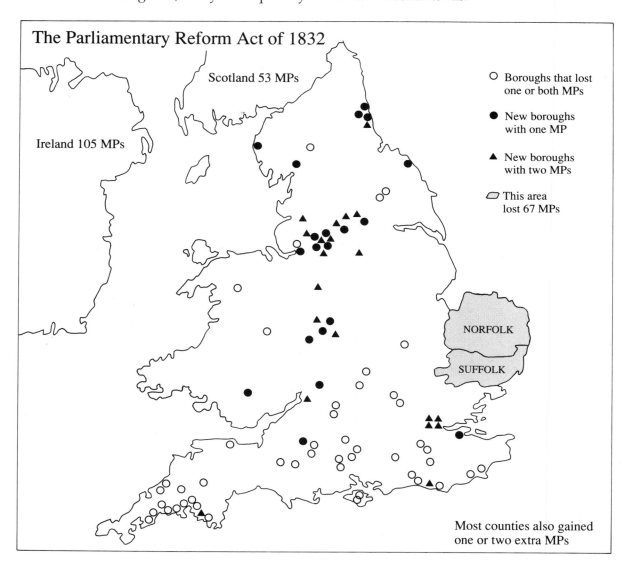

The Parliamentary Reform Act of 1832

Scotland 53 MPs

Ireland 105 MPs

○ Boroughs that lost one or both MPs

● New boroughs with one MP

▲ New boroughs with two MPs

▱ This area lost 67 MPs

NORFOLK

SUFFOLK

Most counties also gained one or two extra MPs

handful of voters they could bribe or intimidate. Voting was not secret but took place in public. Bribery was normal.

There were three political groups:

- *TORIES (in power 1807–1830). Closely allied to the Church of England, the Army, the landed aristocracy and the Royal Family. They included reactionaries opposed to any change and 'Liberal Tories' who would accept gradual reform.*
- *WHIGS (came to power in 1830). More sympathetic than the Tories to reform, and supported by Nonconformists, Catholics and the new industrial middle classes.*
- *RADICALS. A small but active group campaigning for change and more rights, including the vote, for the working class.*

The Duke of Wellington, Tory prime minister 1828–30, opposed electoral reform because he thought that it was unnecessary:

> *I am convinced that the country possesses at the present moment a legislature which answers all the good purposes of legislation . . . I will go further and say that legislature and the system of representation possess the full and entire confidence of the country.*[41]

Who do you think would have disagreed with the Duke?

This Hogarth cartoon shows open bribery at an eighteenth-century election. Voters expected to be bribed or treated in return for their vote. Parliament was certainly not representative of the people as a whole.

During the early 1830s there was enormous pressure for electoral reform. The agitation included serious disturbances and a riot in Bristol that left twelve people dead. Some people, such as the Whig, Lord Macaulay, warned of a revolution if some reforms were not 'speedily adopted':

> *We drive over to the side of revolution those whom we shut out from power.*[42]

The actual reform, passed in 1832, was modest. Rotten boroughs were abolished and representation given to the industrial cities. But the electorate was increased to only 657,000 and, although it now included the middle class, most men and all women remained excluded. What do you think that radical politicians meant when they criticized the Reform Act for being, 'most illiberal and tyrannical, a damnable delusion giving us as many tyrants as there are shop-keepers'? [43]

The sense of betrayal among the working class contributed to the popularity of the Chartist movement a few years later.

Early trade unions

In an industrial society, trade unions exist to protect the interests of the workers. In 1799 and 1800 the government had banned early trade unions by the Combination Acts (which forbade the combination of workers in unions). When these Acts were repealed in 1824 many small unions emerged, though their members were rarely able to take successful strike action.

The first large-scale union was founded in 1834 by Robert Owen, a radical mill owner. He set out to recruit workers from all industries into a single union that would be too powerful to be defeated by employers or the government. Working-class people were now more conscious of the need to unite in their fight for better wages and conditions; in a few weeks Owen's union, the Grand National Consolidated Trades Union (GNCTU), claimed half a million members.

The government was alarmed and, although unions were legal, it sought ways to crush the GNCTU. It turned to an obscure law from 1797 which forbade people to take 'unlawful oaths'. On 10 March 1834 the home secretary suggested that this law could be

After a great public campaign the Tolpuddle Martyrs were released and returned to England in 1836. However, their arrest and transportation showed how hostile the government was to trade unionism.

Robert Owen believed that trade union ineffectiveness resulted from the division of the workers into many small unions. He tried to unite the working class into a single, large union.

used by the government in order to prosecute trade unionists:

Various societies called Trade Unions are at this time spreading . . . At the meeting of these societies secret oaths not to divulge or make known the proceedings of the meeting are administered.[44]

Why do you think that trade unionists met in great secrecy?

In the small Dorset village of Tolpuddle some labourers decided to join the GNCTU and took the oath of secrecy about the society. The local farmers had not kept a promise to raise their workers' wages to ten shillings a week. Instead, the farmers reduced wages to seven shillings a week. In desperation, the labourers turned to a local man, George Loveless, to lead them:

Why should we not form a trade union, we know it is vain to seek redress from employers, magistrates or parsons.[45]

A short time later, Loveless and five others were arrested and charged with taking an illegal oath. This was Loveless's defence:

My Lord, if we have violated any law, it was not done intentionally; we have injured no man's reputation, character, person or property: we were uniting together to preserve ourselves, our wives and our children, from utter degradation and starvation.[46]

In spite of this defence, the Tolpuddle Martyrs, as they became known, were sentenced to seven years' transportation to the chain gangs in Australia. How do you think other supporters of the GNCTU felt when they heard about the arrests at Tolpuddle?

The sentence was a severe blow to the union and its support quickly declined. Internal disagreements and lack of funds also damaged the GNCTU and made any union activity almost useless. The lesson from the 'Black Year' of 1834 was that working-class people would have to seek ways other than trade unions of improving their conditions.

Chartism

Working-class reformers were desperately disappointed by the 1832 Reform Act, the harsh new Poor Law and the collapse of the GNCTU. Out of these setbacks grew a new working-class movement, Chartism.

Chartists were the first working-class group to seek political power. They did not want to overthrow parliamentary government but, through the demands of their People's Charter, they strove to gain the right for working-class people to participate in the government of the country. These were the six points of the Charter:

- *Votes for all men over twenty-one years of age.*
- *A secret ballot.*
- *No property qualification for MPs, so that working men could stand for election.*
- *Payment of MPs.*
- *Constituencies of equal size, so that each MP would represent roughly the same number of people.*
- *Annual parliaments to make MPs more accountable to their constituents.*

A huge procession accompanied the second Chartist petition to the House of Commons in 1842.

Leading Chartists attacked the composition of parliament:

What a farce the present system is! The present House of Commons does not represent the people, but only those fellows who live by usury [moneylending] – a rascally crew who have no real interest in the welfare of the country.[47]

The Chartists tried to win mass support for their aims, and in 1839 and 1842 they presented huge petitions to parliament believing that the moral force of their case would win. Both petitions were overwhelmingly rejected[48]:

Number of Signatures		MPs For	MPs Against
1839	1,250,000	46	235
1842	3,000,000	49	287

What do these figures suggest about the mood of the country compared with that of the House of Commons?

After the first rejection of the Charter, some Chartists, led by Feargus O'Connor, turned to physical force with the slogan, 'Peacefully if

Why is the Charter drawn so large in this cartoon? What is meant by the caption? Do you think the Chartist's demands were reasonable?

we may, forcibly if we must'.[49] The authorities acted firmly against them. Disturbances at Newport, South Wales, left twenty-four people dead and many Chartist leaders were imprisoned.

The final, unsuccessful Chartist demonstration took place at Kennington Common, London, in April 1848. O'Connor had planned to lead a massive crowd of half a million supporters to deliver a third petition with six million signatures to parliament. Yet Chartism's popularity was already on the wane. On the day, only about 20,000 Chartists turned up and the petition contained fewer than two million signatures, many of them apparent forgeries.

Historians argue over the significance of Chartism. Some claim that it was really only a 'bread and butter' or a 'knife and fork' issue; people supported political reform in the hope of improving their standards of living. Other historians emphasize that although Chartism never achieved its aims, it marked, none the less, an important move towards democracy. Chartism had struggled to extend the vote to working-class people:

> *It failed. But it was a necessary step in working-class development . . . It has bequeathed a very real inspiration to subsequent generations.*[50]

43

Public health

As the industrial towns continued to grow, people became more concerned about the unhealthy conditions which existed in them. This is how one 1849 newspaper described a neighbourhood in Leeds:

> The whole vicinity was two or three inches deep in filth . . . In the centre was a cluster of pigsties, privies and cesspools, bursting with pent-up abominations; and a half-dozen paces from this delectable nucleus was a pit about five feet square filled to the very brim with semi-liquid manure.[51]

▲ A major cause of disease was the lack of proper sanitation. Open sewers, such as the Fleet Ditch, flowed through working-class districts of London.

▶ Although Chadwick's report shocked many people with its detailed description of the unhealthy conditions in the cities, parliament was reluctant to take any effective actions.

What would have been the effects of living in conditions like these? What can you tell from the table of figures below, which compares the average age of death in the city of Manchester with that in rural Rutland?

Average Ages of Death in 1842 [52]

	Manchester	Rutland
Professional Persons	38	52
Farmers and Tradesmen	20	41
Mechanics and Labourers	17	38

Edwin Chadwick, secretary to the Poor Law Commission, recognized the link between poverty and illness in the new towns. He was largely responsible for a *Report on the Sanitary Conditions of the Labouring Population*, which was published in 1842. Chadwick identified these main problems:

REPORT

TO

HER MAJESTY'S PRINCIPAL SECRETARY OF STATE FOR THE HOME DEPARTMENT,

FROM THE

POOR LAW COMMISSIONERS,

ON AN INQUIRY INTO THE

SANITARY CONDITION

OF THE

LABOURING POPULATION OF GREAT BRITAIN;

WITH

APPENDICES.

Presented to both Houses of Parliament, by Command of Her Majesty. July, 1842.

LONDON:
PRINTED BY W. CLOWES AND SONS, STAMFORD STREET, FOR HER MAJESTY'S STATIONERY OFFICE.
—
1842.

A COURT FOR KING CHOLERA.

How many causes of disease can you see in this cartoon? Why was parliament slow to act against these causes?

- *No collection or disposal of refuse.*
- *Lack of sewers and use of open cesspools.*
- *No proper supply of clean water.*
- *Lack of clean, fresh air.*
- *Poor burial grounds that contaminated drinking water.*

Chadwick made this conclusion:

> *The annual loss of life from filth and bad ventilation is greater than the loss from death or wounds in any wars in which this country has been engaged in modern times.*[53]

In spite of Chadwick's report, parliament continued to adhere to its *laissez-faire* policy of doing and spending as little as possible on public health. Local government reform in 1835 had set up new town councils, but they had only limited powers to improve conditions. A central Board of Health was founded in 1848, after a severe cholera epidemic, but even its work was restricted.

Why do you think the government was so reluctant to spend money on public health? Some historians blame vested interests for the continuing poor sanitation in towns:

> *Landowners objected that they would have to pay for improvements in towns when they themselves lived elsewhere. Water companies, burial companies, gas companies, builders, proprietors of slum dwellings and others whose profits came from existing conditions opposed change.*[54]

Look again at the figures above, which show the ages of death of different social groups. Were working-class people the only ones to suffer from the middle-class government's refusal to spend more money on public health?

Not until the 1875 Public Health Act were central and local government at last given the powers to tackle effectively the problems of poor sewerage and water supplies.

The Corn Laws

In 1815, the British government had introduced the Corn Laws, which put a tax on imported corn and so kept British corn prices high to the advantage of farmers and landowners. However, many people bitterly resented the tax. Working-class people opposed it because it kept bread prices high, while the middle classes saw the Corn Laws as an obstacle to free trade with other nations.

In 1839 a group of industrialists, particularly textile manufacturers, founded the Anti-Corn Law League in Manchester. Because it was a wealthy, middle-class organization, the League could campaign in ways not available to working-class movements such as the Chartists. ACLL speakers travelled around the country using the new railways; propaganda was sent by penny post to every voter. Before general elections, middle-class voters were urged to support ACLL candidates such as Richard Cobden and John Bright, who both became very effective MPs. Bright was always forthright:

> This House [of Commons] is a club of landowners legislating for landowners. The Corn Law you cherish is a law to make scarcity of food in the country [so] that your own rents may be increased. The quarrel is between the bread-eating millions and the few who monopolise soil.[55]

The ACLL represented first and foremost the interests of middle-class manufacturers at odds with the landed gentry. Yet Bright also appealed to working-class people who were keen that the price of bread should be reduced.

The issue of the Corn Laws finally came to a head in 1845–6, when a virus destroyed much of the potato crop in Ireland (then still part of the United Kingdom). The majority of Irish people depended on potatoes, and crop failure led to the deaths of one million people in a terrible famine.

The Conservative government under Sir Robert Peel was committed to retaining the Corn Laws. However, Peel himself was becoming increasingly sympathetic to the ACLL. When he learned of the Irish potato crop failure, Peel urged his colleagues to support repeal so that cheap food could be imported to Ireland. Many of the landowners in the Tory Party were horrified and convinced that British agriculture would

UP GOES THE QUARTERN LOAF.

Derby. "Now, Gents, Give us only a Little Encouragement—Say a Five Shilling Duty—and 'UP' Goes the Quartern Loaf!"

◀ In 1842 the Corn Laws were reformed in order to reduce the tax on corn. However, the duty on corn still kept the price of bread artificially high and there was widespread distress and protest.

▶ This ACLL propaganda presents the case that prosperity would result from free trade and that the repeal of the Corn Laws would answer the 'people's prayer'. How many reasons for repeal can you see illustrated here?

be ruined overnight. The Duke of Wellington strongly disagreed with Peel:

> *I am one of those who think the continuance of the Corn Laws essential to the agriculture of the country.*[56]

At last, after much argument, the Corn Laws were repealed in June 1846. It was too late to avert tragedy in Ireland, though many people welcomed repeal as a major step forward in free trade.

Within the Tory Party itself, the repeal of the Corn Laws caused much bitterness. However, the fears of the landowners proved to have been ill-founded; agriculture flourished and enjoyed a 'Golden Age', and no attempt was ever made to reintroduce the Corn Laws.

Reform of working conditions

In spite of the huge growth in the number of factory workers, parliament was reluctant to regulate working conditions. No laws were passed during the whole of the nineteenth century to limit the working hours of men, on the grounds that such laws would interfere with the liberty of employers and workers to negotiate over hours and wages.

However, some people felt that women and children should be protected. In 1830 Richard Oastler compared the plight of child factory workers to slaves:

> *Thousands of our fellow-creatures . . . are this very moment existing in a state of slavery, more horrid than are the victims of that hellish system 'colonial slavery'.*[57]

Slavery in British colonies was abolished in 1833, after a campaign that had been supported by many middle-class people. How do you think factory owners reacted to Oastler's accusation?

To protect women and children working in the textile industry, three factory acts were passed:

* *1833 Factory Act*
No children under the age of nine to be employed; *nine- to thirteen-year-olds to work no more than nine hours a day (forty-eight in a week); thirteen- to eighteen-year-olds to work no more than twelve hours a day (sixty-nine in a week); no night work under the age of eighteen; four factory inspectors appointed. However, at first there was no way of proving how old the children were.*

▲ Richard Oastler, a Tory and leader of the Ten Hours Movement, campaigned to restrict the factory working day to ten hours.

◀ This cartoon highlights the problem of factory discipline, which was often harsh and brutal. Fines were imposed on workers for being late, talking or even for opening a window.

• *1844 Factory Act*
Eight- to thirteen-year-olds to work no more than six-and-a-half hours a day and to receive three hours of schooling five times a week; young persons and women limited to twelve hours work a day.

• *1847 Ten Hours Act*
Women and young persons to work no more than ten hours a day.

In 1842 women and boys were also prohibited from working underground in the mines. Compulsory registration of births started in 1836 so that children's ages could be checked.

Although these restrictions may not seem very severe by modern standards, they did arouse opposition. Many women and children lost income because of the new laws, and reforms that were intended to help them sometimes increased hardship. Many factory owners also resisted reform. They argued that they would be unable to compete with foreign industries and would go bankrupt. In the House of Commons, the radical MP William Cobbett argued sarcastically against this claim:

> . . . *a most surprising discovery has been made that all our greatness and prosperity, that our superiority over other nations, is owing to 300, 000 little girls in Lancashire. We have made the notable discovery, that, if these little girls work two hours less in a day than they now do, it would occasion the ruin of the country.*[58]

Do you think Cobbett was right to suggest that limiting the working hours of women and children would not damage industry?

Lord Ashley visited the coal mines himself before introducing the 1842 Mines Act.

6
WORKSHOP OF THE WORLD
The Great Exhibition

THE GREAT EXHIBITION of 1851 celebrated one hundred years of industrial progress. It was suggested by Queen Victoria's husband, Prince Albert, who proposed a 'Great Exhibition of the Works of Industry of all Nations':

> . . . to present a true test and living picture of the point of development at which the whole of mankind has arrived and a new starting point, from which all nations will be able to direct their further exertions.[59]

The exhibition was housed in the Crystal Palace, a huge glass building, designed by Joseph Paxton. The structure contained over 300,000 metres of glass, 3,300 columns and 2,300 girders. On one day alone the exhibition coped with 93,244 visitors. Queen Victoria was thrilled by, 'the beauty of the building and the vastness of it all'.[60]

Exhibitors came from all over the world, but it was British steam-powered machines and inventions that attracted most interest. Visitors also saw the new marvel of the electric telegraph and a huge twelve-metre model of Liverpool Docks. The new railway system brought thousands on their first, and perhaps only, visit to London.

The exhibition was a demonstration of the enormous self-confidence of Victorian Britain. The organizers were convinced that British industry led the way; few Britons in 1851 feared foreign competition in manufactured goods or engineering. The exhibition also demonstrated Britain's commitment to free trade, which, it was thought, would increase wealth. Some people even believed that, by bringing nations closer together, free trade would help preserve peace.

The year 1851 was an appropriate time to look back and take stock of what had been achieved and how the nation had changed. No one could doubt that the upheaval of the

More than six million people visited the Great Exhibition during the six months it was open at the Crystal Palace in Hyde Park.

Industrial Revolution had created a strong and wealthy nation that could, given the will, resolve many social and economic problems.

Yet for all its self-satisfaction and national pride, Britain still had no effective legislation to tackle such problems as public health and poor working conditions. Ironically, Prince Albert was to die in 1861 from typhoid fever contracted, it was said, as a result of the inadequate sanitary conditions at Windsor Castle. Some critics also pointed out that many of the people who flocked to see evidence of Britain's progress at the Great Exhibition themselves lived in slums and worked in sweatshops.

In the half-century following the Great Exhibition, the power and affluence of Britain continued to grow. Yet other countries also now began to experience industrialization. Helped in part by British machinery, Germany and the USA in particular developed industry. In 1851 few Victorians would have foreseen that, by the end of the century, these nations would overtake Britain in some manufacturing industries and rival it as a world power.

Seven thousand exhibitors demonstrated Britain's material prosperity and industrial achievements. The machinery court with its massive hydraulic press and steam-driven machines was the most popular part of the exhibition.

Leading figures

Richard Arkwright (1732–1792)

Arkwright began life as a barber, but devoted himself to improving cotton-spinning processes; he appears to have poached the ideas of others to develop the highly successful water-frame spinning machine. His considerable business skill and organizing ability led to his setting up a water-powered mill in 1771. This mill is generally acknowledged to have been the first example of the modern factory system. However, he faced considerable opposition from the hand workers who saw their livelihood destroyed by his machines and in 1779 one of his factories was destroyed by rioters. He received a knighthood in 1786.

James Brindley proved that canals could be built and operated profitably. Canals were vital to the Industrial Revolution before the coming of the railways.

John Bright (1811–1889)

A Quaker and son of a Lancashire cotton manufacturer, Bright joined the Anti-Corn Law League in 1841, and in 1843 entered parliament as a radical. He campaigned passionately for the repeal of taxes on imported grain, believing that free trade was an important way of preserving peace between nations. After the repeal of the Corn Laws, he remained an MP for most of his life and was also a keen campaigner for electoral reform and the abolition of the death penalty.

James Brindley (1716–1772)

Brindley was an engineer with little formal education when he was commissioned by the

Elizabeth Gaskell's novels give a vivid impression of life in Victorian Britain.

Duke of Bridgewater to construct a canal between Worsley and Manchester in 1759. The success of this canal marked the beginning of the canal age, and Brindley himself went on to build about 560 kilometres of canals. He overcame many difficulties in canal construction by the use of aqueducts and tunnels. He was hailed by many of his contemporaries as a genius who revolutionized transport.

Edwin Chadwick (1801–1890)

Trained as a lawyer, Chadwick was an enthusiastic reformer who was committed to creating cheap and efficient public administration. He drew up the much-hated 1834 Poor Law Act and was responsible for introducing the workhouse system. Yet he also influenced the 1833 Factory Act and battled long and hard to improve public health in towns. Chadwick's arrogant and hectoring manner made him unpopular with many local authorities; nevertheless, his ideas and reports led to several important reforms.

Elizabeth Gaskell (1810–1865)

Elizabeth Gaskell was a novelist who was praised and encouraged to write by Charles Dickens. In 1832 she married a minister and moved to industrial Manchester, where her experiences provided the background for her novels *Mary Barton* (1848) and *North and South* (1855). In 1857 she also wrote a biography of her friend Charlotte Brontë, which attracted some criticism because of its frankness and honesty. Although much of Elizabeth Gaskell's work portrays life in an industrial city, she was not so much a social reformer as someone concerned simply with the kindness of human beings towards each other.

Feargus O'Connor led the militant northern Chartists. Even though he was unsuccessful and died in an asylum, fifty thousand people attended his funeral.

Feargus O'Connor (1794–1855)

Born in Ireland, O'Connor became the leader of those Chartists who believed that they would gain the rights they demanded only through the threat or use of force. Peaceful Chartists blamed him for dividing the movement and alienating middle-class support. However, through his paper, the *Northern Star*, and his fiery speeches O'Connor attracted a considerable following among the working class. His supporters succeeded in electing him to parliament but after the failure of the third Chartist petition he went insane. In 1853 he was forcibly removed from the House of Commons to an asylum where he died two years later.

Robert Owen (1771–1858)

Starting life as a draper's assistant, Owen married a factory owner's daughter, and, with partners, took over his father-in-law's New Lanark Mills in 1800. Owen was an enlightened employer, providing good conditions, shorter hours and reasonable wages for his workers. A strong advocate of co-operative principles, he tried unsuccessfully to set up co-operative shops and factories. His most ambitious project was the Grand National Consolidated Trades Union, founded in 1834, but its radicalism frightened the government and the movement was outlawed. Owen's real achievement was that his ideas, particularly on co-operation, survived to encourage others.

Robert Peel (1788–1850)

Peel entered parliament at the age of twenty-one as the MP for a pocket borough. He became home secretary in 1822, creating the Metropolitan Police Force which was the model for all modern police forces. In 1841 he became prime minister and, although a Tory, was gradually converted to the principles of free trade. He eventually defied his Tory supporters by abolishing the Corn Laws, helped by his close colleague and supporter William Gladstone. Peel died after falling off his horse in Hyde Park.

James Watt (1736–1819)

Watt was a Scottish engineer and instrument-maker. He made a number of improvements to the design of the steam-engine which made possible its widespread use in coal mines and factories. Watt also devised a 'sun and planet' gear to transfer to-and-fro motion into rotary movement. This gear meant that the steam-engine could be used to drive factory machines as well as for pumping. Watt's work was crucial to the Industrial Revolution because he provided an efficient form of power. The term 'watt', for a unit of electrical power is taken from his name.

Mary Wollstonecraft (1759–1797)

Mary Wollstonecraft was a self-educated woman, who, in 1792, caused a sensation with her book, *A Vindication of the Rights of Women*. In it, she argued that women should have the same rights and opportunities as men. 'How many women waste life away,' she wrote, 'the prey of discontent, who might have practised as physicians, regulated a farm, managed a shop?' At the time there were few people who agreed with her and she was denounced as a 'hyena in petticoats'. More recently she has been described as the first feminist. She died in 1797 after giving birth to a baby daughter, Mary, who grew up to become a writer herself and the author of the novel, *Frankenstein*.

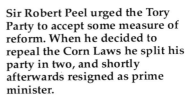

Sir Robert Peel urged the Tory Party to accept some measure of reform. When he decided to repeal the Corn Laws he split his party in two, and shortly afterwards resigned as prime minister.

Important dates

Date	Events
1761	The Duke of Bridgewater's canal between Worsley and Manchester opened.
1764	James Hargreaves invents the spinning jenny.
1766	Building started on the Grand Trunk Canal project.
1769	Use of the water-frame spinning machine by Richard Arkwright.
1776	The thirteen states of America declare independence from Britain.
1779	Samuel Crompton invents the spinning mule.
	Abraham Darby casts the world's first iron bridge at Coalbrookdale.
1783	Montgolfier brothers make the first flight by hot air balloon in Paris.
	Britain recognizes American independence.
1784	Henry Cort develops the puddling process.
	James Watt improves the steam-engine.
1785	Edmund Cartwright invents the power loom.
1786	Threshing machine invented.
1789	French Revolution begins.
1793	Beginning of Britain's wars with revolutionary France.
1795	Introduction of the Speenhamland system of poor relief.
1798	Publication of Malthus's *Essay on the Principle of Population*.
1801	First population census taken.
1802	The first successful steamship, the *Charlotte Dundas,* launched.
1805	Grand Junction Canal completed.
1807	Slave trade abolished in the British Empire.
1811	Luddite machine-breaking starts.
1812	Assassination of the prime minister, Spencer Perceval.
1815	Battle of Waterloo and the end of wars with France.
	Introduction of the Corn Laws.
	Humphrey Davy invents the miner's safety lamp.
1819	'Peterloo' massacre in Manchester.
	Introduction of the Six Acts to limit working-class protest.
1825	George Stephenson completes the Stockton to Darlington railway line.
1829	Robert Peel forms the Metropolitan Police.
1830	Liverpool to Manchester railway line built by George and Robert Stephenson.
	Revolutionary movements in France, Germany, Poland and Italy.
1831	Serious cholera epidemic.
1832	First Parliamentary Reform Act.
1833	Abolition of slavery in the British Empire.
	First Factory Act to restrict the working hours of women and children.
1834	Poor Law Amendment Act and introduction of the workhouse system.
	Conviction of the Tolpuddle martyrs and collapse of the GNCTU.
1835	Municipal Reform Act alters local government.
	The term 'socialism' first used.
1836	The *People's Charter* expresses the demands of the Chartist movement.
1837	Queen Victoria accedes to the throne.
1839	First Chartist petition presented to parliament.
	Queen Victoria marries Prince Albert.

Date	Events
1842	Second Chartist petition presented to parliament. Chadwick's report on public health in towns. Mines Act bans women and children from working underground.
1844	Railway Act; 'railway mania' begins. Factory Act to further limit the working hours of women and children. Electric telegraph perfected by Samuel Morse in the USA.
1845–6	Irish potato famine.
1846	Repeal of the Corn Laws. Sewing machine invented in the USA. Disraeli's *Sybil* published.
1847	Factory Act limits the working day for women and young people to ten hours.
1848	Final Chartist petition presented to parliament. Revolutions in several European countries.
1851	The Great Exhibition.

Glossary

Capitalist	A person who invests capital (money) in industry in order to receive a share of the profits.
Capital offence	Crime for which the punishment is death.
Census	A count of the population. A population census has taken place in Britain every ten years since 1801 (except in 1941).
Cholera	Fatal disease caused by drinking water that has been contaminated by sewage.
Croppers	People who 'cropped', or trimmed, the finished cloth in the woollen industry.
Democracy	A political system in which the government is chosen by the people.
Domestic system	Manufacture of goods inside people's homes. This was the main system of manufacture before the introduction of the factory system.
Emancipation	Making someone free, usually by granting them equal rights.
Enclosure	The process of fencing in land, making small, enclosed fields out of large, open ones.
Entrepreneur	Someone who raises capital (money) and recruits workers in order to set up a new business.
Fallow	Farmland that is left unused for a season so that it will not lose its fertility by being over-cultivated.
Feminist	Someone who supports rights for women.
Free trade	The system of trade in which no barriers such as taxes or duties on goods exist between nations.
Hosiery trade	The industry which makes stockings.
Improvidence	Being careless with money or foolishly spending one's wealth.
Industrialization	The development of industry on a large scale.
Jerry-built	Badly built, using poor quality material.
Justice of the Peace	A magistrate responsible for administering the law. Justices of the Peace were often very powerful in the eighteenth and nineteenth centuries.
Laissez-faire	The policy of government interfering as little as possible in trade and industry.
Legislature	The person or group of people which makes laws. In Britain, parliament is the legislature.
Less eligibility	The principle by which the conditions of people in workhouses were deliberately kept worse than those of the poorest people outside.
Nitrates	Chemicals in soil that are needed for crops to grow.
Nonconformist	In Britain, a Protestant, such as a Methodist, who is not a member of the established, Anglican Church.
Pig iron	Bars of rough iron.
Pocket borough	A parliamentary constituency before the Great Reform Act, in which one powerful landowner could decide who would be the MP.
Privy	A lavatory, usually outside.
Puddling	A method of making iron so that it can be formed into shapes.
Putter	Usually a woman or young person who pulled or carried baskets of coal in the mines.

Radical	Nineteenth-century politician who campaigned to extend the right to vote and for social reform on behalf of the working class.
Reactionary	Opposed to change and wanting to return to the way things were.
Rotten borough	A parliamentary constituency before the Great Reform Act, in which only a very small number of people elected the MP.
Sedition	Plotting against the government.
Smallholding	A small farm or piece of farmland.
Smelting	Extracting a metal from its ore or natural state.
Social group	A group of people within society, such as the factory workers or the landowners.
Socialism	Political system based on equal distribution of wealth, good provision of welfare benefits and state ownership of industry.
Subsistence	The basic things needed (e.g., money, food and clothing) for survival.
Tory Party	The political party of the landed aristocracy. It began to adopt the name Conservative after 1834.
Trade union	An organization to protect the interests of the workers in a particular industry.
Transportation	Punishment of criminals by sending them to colonies overseas. In the nineteenth century, British criminals were usually transported to Australia.
Turnpike	A road that people pay to use.
Usury	Lending money at a very high rate of interest.
Vested interests	A strong personal concern in something.
Whigs	The political party that advocated some modest reform and was replaced by the Liberal Party.

Further reading

Textbooks
Catchpole, B., *A Map History of the British People Since 1700*, Heinemann, 1983.
Cootes, R.J., *Britain Since 1700*, Longman, 1983.
Culpin, C. and Turner, B., *Making Modern Britain*, Longman, 1986.
Reynoldson, F., *Agriculture Since 1700*, Heinemann, 1990.
Robottom, J., *A Social and Economic History of Industrial Britain*, Longman, 1986.
Sauvain, P., *British Economic and Social History 1700–1870*, Stanley Thornes, 1987.
Speed, P.F., *British Social and Economic History*, Wheaton, 1977.
Unwin, R., *Britain Since 1700*, Hutchinson, 1986.

Scholarly Books
Briggs, A., *The Age of Improvement*, Longman, 1979.
Court, W.H.B., *A Concise Economic History of Britain*, Cambridge University Press, 1954.
Harrison, J.F.C., *Early Victorian Britain 1832–51*, Fontana, 1979.
Hunt, E.H., *British Labour History 1815–1914*, Weidenfeld & Nicolson, 1981.
Gregg, P., *A Social and Economic History of Britain 1760–1980*, Harrap, 1982.
Mathias, P., *The First Industrial Nation*, Methuen, 1969.
May, T., *An Economic and Social History of Britain 1760–1979*, Longman, 1987.
Pinchbeck, I., *Women Workers and the Industrial Revolution 1750–1850*, Virago, 1981.
Thompson, E. P., *The Making of the English Working Class*, Penguin, 1968.

Contemporary Novels
Brontë, C., *Shirley*, (first published 1849), Oxford University Press, 1981.
Dickens, C., *The Adventures of Oliver Twist*, (first published 1838), Oxford University Press, 1982.
Disraeli, B., *Sybil*, (first published 1848), Oxford University Press, 1981.
Gaskell, E., *Mary Barton*, (first published 1848), Oxford University Press, 1987.
Kingsley, C., *Alton Locke, Tailor and Poet*, (first published 1850), Oxford University Press, 1985.

Notes on sources

1 Porter, G.R., *Progress of the Nation*, 1847.
2 Cook, C. and Keith, B., *British Historical Facts 1800–1900*, Macmillan, London, 1975.
3 Deane, P. and Mitchell, B.R., *Abstract of British Historical Statistics*, Cambridge University Press, Cambridge, 1960.
4 Wesley, John, *Sermons*, 1778.
5 Malthus, Thomas, *Essay on the Principle of Population*, 1798.
6 Cited in Plumb, J.H., *England in the Eighteenth Century*, Penguin, Middlesex, 1950.
7 Young, Arthur, *Annals of Agriculture*, 1797.
8 Cited in Wallace, R., *Farm Livestock in Great Britain*, 1907.
9 Cited in Robottom, J., *A Social and Economic History of Industrial Britain*, Longman, Essex, 1986.
10 Arthur Young, cited in Briggs, A., *The Age of Improvement*, Longman, Essex, 1979.
11 Dunckley, H., *The Charter of the Nations*, 1854.
12 Ashton, T.S., *The Industrial Revolution 1760–1830*, Oxford University Press, Oxford, 1968.
13 Plumb *op. cit.*
14 Cited in Harvie, C., *The Industrial Revolution*, Open University Press, Milton Keynes, 1972.
15 Gregg, P., *A Social and Economic History of Britain 1760–1980*, Harrap, London, 1982.
16 Cited in Thompson, E.P., *The Making of the English Working Class*, Penguin, Middlesex, 1968.
17 Deane and Mitchell, *op. cit.*
18 Cited in Pinchbeck, I., *Women Workers and the Industrial Revolution*, Virago, London, 1981.
19 Cited in Reeve, R.M., *The Industrial Revolution 1750–1850*, University of London Press, London, 1971.
20 Cited in Trinder, B., *The Coalbrookdale Museum of Iron*, Ironbridge Gorge Museum Trust, 1979.
21 Pinchbeck, *op. cit.*
22 Cited in Briggs, *op. cit.*
23 Engels, F., *The Condition of the Working Class in England*, George Allen & Unwin, London, 1892.
24 Cited in Briggs, *op. cit.*
25 Court, W.H.B., *A Concise Economic History of Britain*, Cambridge University Press, Cambridge, 1954.
26 Cited in May, T., *An Economic and Social History of Britain 1760–1970*, Longman, 1987.
27 Simmons, J., *The Railways in England and Wales 1830–1914*, A. & C. Black, 1978.
28 Briggs, *op.cit.*
29 Disraeli, Benjamin, *Sybil*, 1846.
30 Cited in Hobsbawn, E.J., *The Age of Revolution 1789–1848*, Weidenfeld & Nicolson, London, 1962.
31 Engels, *op. cit.*
32 Cited in Briggs, A., *Victorian Cities*, Odhams, 1963.
33 Cited in Griswick, J. (ed.), *Labour and the Poor in England and Wales 1849–1851*, Frank Cass, London, 1983.
34 *The Times*, 1 August 1854.
35 Pinchbeck, *op.cit.*
36 *Ibid.*
37 *Ibid.*
38 Cited in Gregg, *op.cit.*
39 Cited in Bull, A., *The Machine Breakers*, Collins, London, 1980.
40 Cited in Thompson, *op.cit.*
41 Duke of Wellington in the House of Lords, 2 November 1830.
42 Macaulay in the House of Commons, 2 March 1831.
43 Cited in Seymour, C.S., *Electoral Reform in England and Wales*, New Haven, 1915.
44 Cited in *The Martyrs of Tolpuddle 1834–1934*, Trades Union Congress, London, 1934.
45 *Ibid.*
46 *Ibid.*
47 Cited in Brown, R. and Daniels, C., *The Chartists*, Macmillan, London, 1984.
48 Gregg, *op.cit.*
49 Cited in *ibid.*
50 *Ibid.*
51 Griswick *op.cit.*
52 Extracted from Government Commission *Report on the Sanitary Conditions of the Labouring Population*, 1842.
53 *Ibid.*
54 Gregg, *op.cit.*
55 Cited in O'Brien, R.B., *John Bright*, Thomas Nelson, London, 1910.
56 Cited in Peel, Robert, *Memoirs*, John Murray, London, 1857.
57 Cited in Hollis, P., *Class and Conflict in Nineteenth Century England, 1815–1830*, Routledge and Kegan Paul, 1973.
58 Cited in Gregg *op.cit.*
59 Cited in Briggs, A., *Victorian People*, Penguin, Middlesex, 1965.
60 *Letters of Queen Victoria*, John Murray, London, 1907.

Index

Figures in **bold** refer to illustrations

Picture acknowledgements

The author and publishers would like to thank the following for allowing their illustrations to be reproduced in this book: Communist Party Library 23 (below); E.T. Archive 21, 37, 50; Mary Evans Picture Library 4, 9, 11 (below), 16, 17, 27, 29, 31 (above), 32 (right), 33, 44 (right), 45, 47, 48 (above), 51, 52, 53, 54; Fotomas 5 (below), 30, 32 (left), 34, 43; Ironbridge Gorge Museum cover; Billie Love 12, 23 (above), 25, 31 (below), 44 (left); The Mansell Collection 5 (above), 7, 11 (above), 14, 19 (below), 20, 36, 40, 46; Peter Newark 13 (right), 28, 35, 49; Wayland Picture Library 10, 13 (left), 19 (above), 22, 39, 41, 42, 48 (below), 55. All artwork is by Jenny Hughes.